No. 2652
Wide Brim Plain Black Wool ... made from fine quality Saxony, soft ... 6¾ to 7½. Price, each ... **$0.75**
Wide Brim Planter Hats. Same color. Each ... **$0.75**

... Best Quality Saxony Wool ... brim with ribbon band and bind ... give good service. Color, black. ... **$0.95**
... Hats. Same as above in drab. ... **$0.95**

Ranch Hats.

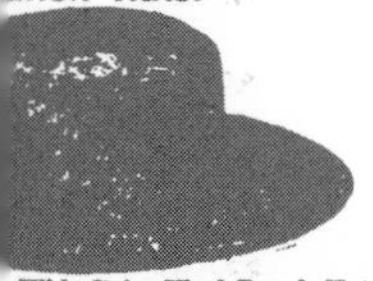

Wide Brim Wool Ranch Hats ... leather sweatband. Nutria or tan 7¼ only. Each ... **$0.50**
... Hats. Made of fine Saxony wool, ... and and leather sweat band, ... and solid service. Sizes, 6¾ to 7½ ... A real bargain. Colors. Price, each ... **$1.00**

... oy's Sombreros.

... Excellent Line of Cow Boy ... They are made from the very ... hand finished with the very best ... and warranted to give perfect ... that has been made with the ... that it must give real and last ... the wearer. We quote only the ... it can at any time have special ... made to order. Special atten ... ted to the fact that it requires ... to have a special hat made to ... re to have a special hat made to ... to us first describing fully the ... being sure to state size, color, ... of crown. etc. The following ... sizes 6¾, 6⅞, 7, 7⅛, 7¼, 7⅜, 7½, ... ave to be made specially to order ... ts to $1.50 extra.

No. 2658
The World Famous J. B. Stetson Sombrero Hat is ... worn by the most famous scout and guide in the world. Made from finest nutria fur stock. Belly nutria color with silk band and binding. Crown 4½ inch; brim 4 inch. Sizes 6¾-7½; weight 6 oz.
Price each ... **$5.00**

No. 2660
The Reservation Sombrero, or Cow Boy's Hat; clear fur stock. Belly nutria color, with silk ribbon band and binding; 4½-inch crown; 4 ... tin lining; heavy leather, sweat ... soft smooth finish; will hold its ... od solid wear. Sizes 6¾ to 7½. ... desired. Price each ... **$3.00**

The Cattle King, $2.50

No. 2667 The Cattle King, cow boy sombrero. Clear nutria fur stock. Belly nutria color. 4½-inch crown; 4-inch brim, with raw edge. Fine soft finish. One inch silk ribbon band. Sizes 6¾ to 7½. One of our specially good things. Guaranteed to give satisfaction. Weight 6 oz. Price, each ... **$2.50**

No. 2668 The Cattle King Sombrero. Same as above, with silk band and binding; weight 6 oz.; sizes 6¾ to 7½. Belly nutria color.
Price, each ... **$2.75**

Buckskin Felt Sombreros.

Nos. 2669-2670.

No. 2669 Cow Boys' Buckskin Felt Sombreros. 4½-inch crown; 4-inch brim, and 1¾-inch leather band. Belly nutria or buckskin color. Raw edge and fine leather sweat band. Sizes 6¾ to 7½. Weight 8 oz. Price, each ... **$2.85**

No. 2670 Cow Boys' Extra Fine Heavy Weight Saxony Wool Sombreros, with 4½-inch crown and 4-inch brim, with wide single buckle embossed leather band and leather binding. The leather band on this hat is a handsome and desirable feature; it is embossed in beautiful floral and novelty patterns in variegated colors; very attractive and handsome. Sizes 6¾ to 7½ only. Color belly nutria or light calfskin. Price, each ... **$1.69**

The Mustang Hat.

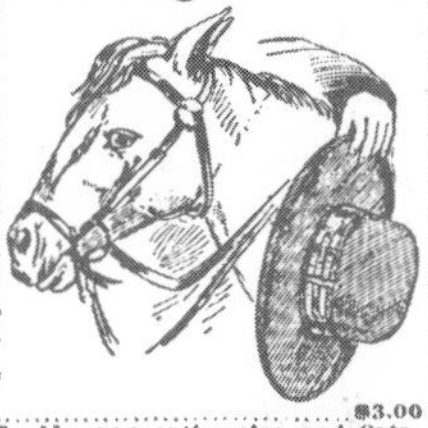

No. 2673 The Mustang. Cow Boy's Buckskin Felt Sombrero. 4½-inch crown, 4 inch brim and 2 inch embossed double buckle; leather band and leather binding, and fancy satin lining. Sizes, 6¾ to 7½. Color, calfskin or buckskin. Weight, 8 oz. Always state size desired.
Price, each ... **$3.00**

IMPORTANT.—Always mention size and Catalogue number when ordering hats of any kind.

No. 2674 The Vaquero. An ideal sombrero. Made from clear nutria fur. Belly nutria color. 4½ inch crown, and 3¾ inch hat air splitting brim. Improved ... leather sweat band and raw edge. Made without lining and with one-inch silk ribbon band. Silk elastic cord and eyelets, which can be attached to the coat, thus avoiding trouble and "cuss words" in case the hat should blow off. Sizes, 6¾ to 7½. Weight, 6 oz. Price, each ... **$3.00**

$2.35 Razor Blade Acme Lawn Mower.

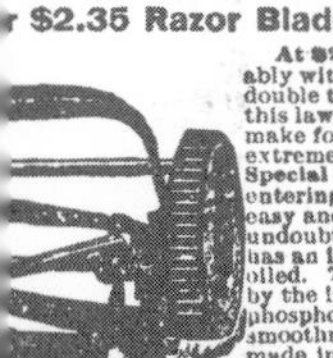

At $2.35 we offer a lawn mower which will compare favorably with any machine you can buy in your local market at double the price. After thorough and exacting tests we offer this lawn mower, confident that it will justify every claim we make for it. It is especially adapted to small lawns. It is extremely light, making it easy to carry from place to place. Special care has been taken in the selection of all the material entering into its construction. Simplicity of construction, easy and accurate operation, durability and finish make this undoubtedly the best light mower on the market. The mower has an improved cutter-bar of solid tool steel, tempered and polled. The knives have a positive shear cut and are regulated by the improved micrometer adjustment. The shafts run in phosphor bronze bearings, adding greatly to the ease and smoothness of running. New malleable iron handle brace made in one piece. Diameter of traction wheel, 7 inches; reel, 5 inches. All parts are interchangeable and can be re ... expense in case of breakage or wear. ... ce of 10-inch, 12-inch, 14-inch or 16-inch ... as your order. ... a 3 per cent. discount if cash in full accompanies your order. ... **$2.35**

... Acme Lawn Mowers At $3.50 to $4.20.

... Mower at $3.50; 18 inch at $3.85 and ... Three per cent. discount allowed if ... as your order. ... and high grade Acme machine and ... r this season. The drive wheels are ... the tread, though the working parts ... oiled. It is the easiest running lawn ... The handle brace is so attached to the

---

No. 2665 Pride of the Platte. A fine soft fur sombrero hat with 4-inch crown and 3½-inch brim with raw edge, and fine 1-inch silk ribbon band. Very popular with cow boys, herdsmen, hunters, vanqueros and planters. Belly nutria color. Sizes 6¾ to 7½. Price each ... **$2.75**

No. 93037, $12.00

No. 93038 Same Saddle with leather covered steel stirrups ... **12.65**
Add for all wool lined chafes and connecting strap on sinches ... **1.00**

Our $13.25 Stock Saddle.

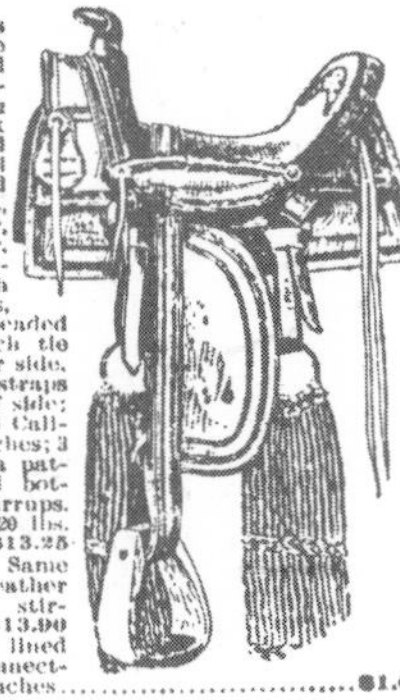

No. 93039 This Saddle is made of genuine oiled California skirting; has a 14½ inch steel fork hide covered tree; 23 in. wool lined skirt solid leather seat, stamped flower, steel strainer, beaded roll cantle; 1⅞ inch stirrup leathers, raised and beaded gullet; 1¼ inch tie straps on near side, 1¼ inch latigo straps to buckle on off side; 20 strand white California hair sinches; 3 inch California pattern leathered bottom and bar stirrups. Weight about 20 lbs. Our price ... **$13.25**

No. 93040 Same Saddle with leather covered steel stirrups ... **$13.90**
Add for wool lined chafes and connecting strap on sinches ... **$1.00**

Our $12.65 Stock Saddle.

No. 93041 (No. 93041L)

No. 93041 This Saddle is made of genuine oiled California skirting; genuine Llama skin housing; seat is solid leather, has steel strainer and roll cantle; 1¾ inch stirrup leathers; 1¼ inch tie straps. Sinches are genuine Mexican string hair; 3 inch California pattern stirrups. Weight about 15 pounds.
Our price ... **$12.65**

No. 93042 Same Saddle, leather covered steel stirrups ... **$13.50**
Add for wool lined chafes and connecting straps on sinches ... **$1.00**

... steel fork hide covered tree; 22¼ inch wool lined skirts; ... solid leather stamped steel beaded roll cantle; 1⅞ inch stirrup leathers raised and beaded gullet; 1¼ inch tie straps on near side, 1¼ inch latigo straps to buckle on off side; 20 strand gray California hair sinches; 3 inch California pattern leathered bar and bottom stirrups. Weight about 19 pounds. Our price ... **$12.00**

No. 93044. Same saddle with leather covered steel stirrups ... **12.65**
Add for all wool lined chafes and connecting strap on sinches ... **1.00**

Our $15.25 Stock Saddle.

No. 93045. This saddle is made of genuine oiled California skirting; has 14½ inch steel fork hide covered tree; 24 inch wool lined skirts. Seat is of solid leather, stamped flower, steel strainer, beaded roll cantle. Stirrup leathers, 2 inch, gullet raised and beaded; tie straps 1½ inch on near side, latigo straps to buckle around 1¾ inch, has genuine Mexican string hair sinches, leathered wool lined and connecting straps, 3 inch California pattern leathered bar and bottom stirrups. Weight about 21 lbs.
Price ... **$15.25**
No. 93046. Same saddle with leather covered steel stirrups ... **$15.90**

Our $16.75 Stock Saddle.

No. 93047. This is an exceptionally fine saddle, made of genuine oiled California skirting. Has a 15 inch steel fork hide covered tree; 24 inch wool lined skirts; seat is solid leather, beaded roll cantle, seat and jockey made in one piece. Has raised and beaded gullet, 2 inch stirrup leathers, 1⅞ inch tie straps. 6 inch Mexican string hair sinches, leathered, wool lined and connecting strap. Has 3 inch California pattern stirrups, leathered top and bottom. Weight about 21 lbs. Our price ... **$16.75**

PHANTOM MINNOWS.

... steel fork hide covered tree; 22¾ inch wool lined skirts; ... Price ... **$13.95**
No. 93044. Same saddle with leather covered steel stirrups ... **$14.60**
Add for wool chafes and connecting strap on sinches ... **$1.00**

... D handle, capped ferrule, Spading Fork, ... steel tines. Price, each, 50c; Per dozen ...
No. 1585 D handle, capped and strapped ferrule, Spading Fork, 4 heavy angular steel tines, strongest and best spading fork made. Price, each ... 60c; Per dozen ...

Coke Forks.

Coke Forks. Made of the best cast steel, strap ferrule. D handle.
No. 1387 Price, each, 10 tooth ...
No. 1388 Price, each, 12 tooth ...
No. 1389 Price, each, 14 tooth ...

Manure and Potato Hooks.

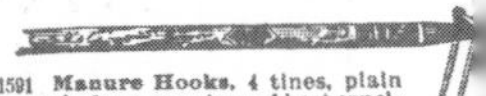

No. 1591 Manure Hooks. 4 tines, plain ferrule, made from one piece of best crucible steel. Each ... 32c

Potato Hooks.

No. 1593 Potato Digger, 4 round tines. Price, each ... 25c; Per dozen ...
No. 1594 Potato Digger, 4 flat tines. Price, each ... 25c; Per dozen ...

Shovel Handles.

No. 1596 Malleable "Da" for fork or shovel handles.
Price, each ... **$0.07**
Per doz ... **0.70**

Get your neighbors interested, and club together for a mixed freight order.

Hay Forks.

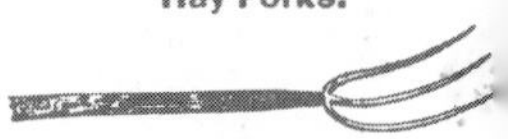

This cut shows the Plain Ferrule. Straight handle, Plain Capped Ferrule Forks, 3 oval tines, standard size and length; ted handles.

	No. 1597	No. 1597	No. 1598	No. 1599
Length of handle, ft..	4	4½	5	5½
Price, each ...	$0.29	$0.29	$0.29	$0.29
Price, dozen ...	3.23	3.25	3.25	3.33

Straight Handle, capped and strapped ferrule Hay Forks, 3 oval tines, standard size and le ... lected handles.

	No. 1605	No. 1606	No. 1606	No. 1607
Length of handle, ft..	4	4½	5	5½
Price, each ...	$0.34	$0.34	$0.34	$0.35
Price, dozen ...	3.75	3.75	3.75	3.87

This cut shows the Strapped Ferrule. Bent handle, plain capped ferrule Hay Forks, 3 oval tines, standard size and length; se ... handles.

	No. 1610	No. 1612	No. 1613	No. 1614
Length of handle, ft..	4	4½	5	5½
Price, each ...	$0.30	$0.30	$0.30	$0.32
Price, dozen ...	3.30	3.36	3.39	3.50

Bent handle, capped and strapped ferrule Forks, 3 oval tines, standard size and length lected handles.

	No. 1618	No. 1620	No. 1621	No. 1622
Length of handle ft..	4	4½	5	5½
Price, each ...	$0.35	$0.35	$0.35	$0.36
Price, dozen ...	3.92	3.92	3.92	4.04

REMEMBER OUR LIBERAL DISCOUNT OF CEN ... When cash in full accompanies ...

Weed Scythe.

No. 1753. Weed Scythes. Extra cast steel. ch ... **$4.50** Per dozen ...

Bush Snath.

No. 1754. Cast Steel Bush Scythe. Price, each, **$0.40**

Grass Snath.

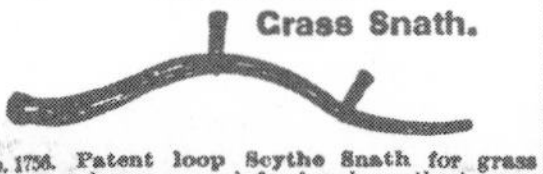

No. 1756. Patent loop Scythe Snath for grass scythes (not heavy enough for brush scythes), complete with wrench. Price, each ... **$0.55**

HELGAMITES.

No. 81725. Helgamite or Dobson soft rubber with swivel. Each, 25c

ARTIFICIAL BAITS.

No. 81726. Bumble bee, cockchafer, beetle, caterpillar, fly-minnow, wasps, blue bottle, lady bird, spider cricket and house fly; assorted colors. Each ... 15c
Grasshopper, small, each ...
Grasshopper, large, each ...

LIFE IN AMERICA 100 YEARS AGO

Frontier Life

LIFE IN AMERICA 100 YEARS AGO

Frontier Life

David Ritchie

Chelsea House Publishers

New York   Philadelphia

CHELSEA HOUSE PUBLISHERS

Editorial Director: Richard Rennert
Executive Managing Editor: Karyn Gullen Browne
Copy Chief: Robin James
Picture Editor: Adrian G. Allen
Creative Director: Robert Mitchell
Art Director: Joan Ferrigno
Production Manager: Sallye Scott

LIFE IN AMERICA 100 YEARS AGO

Senior Editor: Jake Goldberg

Staff for *FRONTIER LIFE*
Editorial Assistant: Erin McKenna
Assistant Designer: Lydia Rivera
Picture Researcher: Sandy Jones
Cover Illustrator: Steve Cieslawski

First Printing

1 3 5 7 9 8 6 4 2

Library of Congress Cataloging-in-Publication Data

Ritchie, David
    Frontier Life/David Ritchie
    p. cm.—(Life in America 100 years ago)
    Includes bibliographical reference and index.
    ISBN 0-7910-2842-9
    1. Frontier and pioneer life—West (U.S.)—Juvenile literature. 2. Country life—West
(U.S.)—History—19th century—Juvenile literature. 3. West (U.S.)—History—Juvenile
literature. [1. Frontier and pioneer life—West (U.S.) 2. West (U.S.)—History.] I. Title. II. Series.
F596.R59 1995   95-6255
978—dc20   CIP
                                                                                                    AC

CONTENTS

LIFE IN AMERICA 100 YEARS AGO

Frontier Life

Industry

Law and Order

Manners and Customs

Health and Medicine

Sports and Recreation

Transportation

Urban Life

Frontier Life

The Frontier

TOM HAMILTON WENT DOWN IN HISTORY, IN A SMALL BUT colorful way, because his pigs made so much trouble in Ehrenberg, Arizona. Hamilton served as merchant, saloon keeper, and justice of the peace in Ehrenberg in the 1860s and 1870s. He also owned a herd of pigs, which he allowed to roam free. The swine annoyed townspeople by entering private homes and stores and eating what they could find.

Hamilton heard so many complaints about his pigs that he knew he would have to do something. He rounded up the pigs, ferried them by raft across the Colorado River to California, and let the animals loose. There, he apparently hoped, the pigs could fend for themselves while staying out of trouble.

Even in exile, however, the pigs caused problems. They devoured the cache of food in a prospector's shack. The prospector retaliated by shooting and butchering one of the pigs. One of Hamilton's employees witnessed this incident and told him about it. To avenge

In Loup Valley, Nebraska, in 1886, a family of westward-bound settlers pose for an unknown photographer in front of their covered wagon. The wagon is a smaller, modified version of the large Conestoga wagons that were used back East to haul freight between Lancaster Valley in Pennsylvania and the cities of Philadelphia and Baltimore. Massachusetts fishermen who went west dubbed them "prairie schooners."

the death of the pig, Hamilton took his gun, made his way across the river, and confronted the prospector.

The prospector knew something about the law and pointed out that Hamilton had no authority there because he was out of his Arizona jurisdiction. "This is California!" the prospector argued. Hamilton replied that his gun gave him all the authority he needed. The prospector was taken into custody and had to appear before justice of the peace Tom Hamilton in court. Hamilton fined the prospector $100—$50 for stealing Hamilton's property, and $50 for killing the pig.

The tale of Tom Hamilton's pigs provides a small but revealing glimpse of frontier life in America during the 19th century. In the rural America of those days, livestock could run free on the streets of towns. The prospector, a now almost legendary figure, then roamed the land in search of mineral wealth. Moreover, the workings of justice were different then from what they are now, so that a justice of the peace—after bringing back a suspect, at gunpoint, from outside his jurisdiction—could preside over the defendant's trial involving the alleged theft of the justice's own property!

As this case demonstrates, frontier life in America during the 1800s was vastly different from American life today. Even rural communities of our time are far removed from the frontier environment of the 1800s. Many of our popular images of 19th-century frontier life bear little resemblance to its realities. Few elements of American history have been more thoroughly romanticized and mythologized than the frontier.

Hardy pioneers making their way by wagon across the plains; close-knit families living in modest but happy homes on the prairie;

This wagon train is bringing farm implements, supplies, and cattle to settlers in the Black Hills of South Dakota, land that had to be cleared of the Sioux by the U.S. Army before it could be extensively settled.

In 1889, in Guthrie, Oklahoma, a settler stakes his claim to a plot of land simply by searching for an empty space in the middle of "town."

exuberant fortune hunters seeking gold in California; cowboys riding the range in merry camaraderie; and all of them enjoying basically unspoiled natural surroundings, free from the environmental woes of the late 20th century—this is how we commonly imagine frontier life to have been 100 years ago.

These images, promulgated by numerous works of literature and entertainment, are partly true and partly false. The question is, how does one separate fact from falsehood? That is not always easy to do. Much information about frontier life has been ignored or forgotten over the years. We know enough, however, to be sure that life then was far from our rosy vision of it today. If you could travel back through time and revisit rural America in the 1800s, you might be shocked at what you found. You might even be too disgusted to shake hands with your own ancestors!

Depending on where you looked, you would find frontier communities ravaged by epidemic disease, beset by economic depression, devastated by crop failure, and crushed under workloads that seem almost unbelievable in our mechanized era. Descriptions of frontier homes are reminiscent of prison camps in some of the more repressive nations of our own time. Living quarters were cramped and malodorous. In a one-room cabin, a family might carry on all the activities of daily life, plus a variety of home industries. When a home became infested with vermin, no pesticides were available to kill them. So the bugs stayed.

By current standards, some frontier settlements were almost as isolated as if they had been located in Antarctica or on the moon. Indeed, the natural environment sometimes must have seemed

In the late 19th century, a farm family has its portrait taken. Neither gunslingers nor adventurers tamed the West, farmers did. At the rate of 30 miles a year, they transformed the wild prairies into productive farmland. It was the farmers who demanded civil administration, the rule of law, statehood, and public education.

The houses of western frontier families were made of sod or stone or bricks. Log cabins were a rarity, because there were few trees on the Great Plains to cut for wood. Early on, horses were a luxury, and most families made do with oxen.

nearly as inhospitable as outer space or the South Pole. Snowfall could literally bury a community. It was not unheard-of for a western settler to have a home with a special door set at the top of a tower so that he could enter and leave over the tops of huge snowdrifts in winter.

This black mother and child, photographed around 1900, were descendants of an African–American family who escaped from slavery and were welcomed into a community of Creek Indians living in the Oklahoma Territory. Though some Native American tribes kept slaves, many black fugitive slaves were taken into their tribes, and intermarriage was common.

Health care on the 19th-century American frontier was primitive and based largely on Native American lore. Antibiotics were nonexistent. The surgeon's art was scarcely advanced over the butcher's. Frontier residents of the 1800s had to cope with illnesses that a modern American is unlikely to encounter, from malaria (then called "ague") to typhoid.

Firearms were widespread, and few restrictions were applied to their use. Death by violence was commonplace. Police departments

15

as we know them were nonexistent. In their absence, "justice" was administered—in many cases at the end of a rope—by vigilantes, or self-appointed vengeance squads.

These sufferings and atrocities took place during a vast struggle for the ownership of western North America. The winners were Americans of European descent. The losers were Native Americans, whose domains had been steadily pushed westward since the early 17th century. That westward movement continued through the 1800s, as whites and blacks surged westward and displaced or destroyed the Native American peoples. This process has been described as the

At a Sunday church service in Kansas, the members of a wagon train gather to reaffirm their commitment to push on to Oklahoma, even though they would be invading Native American land.

The courthouse and town square of Independence, Missouri, around 1855. Independence was the starting point for the Oregon Trail.

"opening of the West," almost as if that part of the continent were some great gift that was to be unwrapped at a special ceremony.

Actually, the West was "opened" in a series of movements that took place over some three centuries. Starting with their initial settlements on the Atlantic coast, the newcomers moved westward despite opposition from Native Americans. The easterners reached the Missouri River before 1850. From there, they continued on their way toward the Pacific.

The pioneers came by many routes. Some crossed the continent by wagon. Others traveled by ship around stormy Cape Horn, at the southern tip of South America, to reach the western shores of North America. Still others sailed to Panama, crossed the narrow isthmus by foot and boat (the Panama Canal did not exist then), and proceeded to sail northward up the Pacific coast. It is difficult to say who must have faced the greater hardships—passengers on a storm-tossed vessel rounding Cape Horn or pioneers making their slow way overland by wagon. The wagons' occupants at least did not risk drowning at sea. Nonetheless, the trip across the continent was hazardous and, for many travelers, their last journey on earth. The overland travelers left behind a trail of wrecked wagons, graves, and the skeletons of livestock along their westward routes.

Perhaps the best known of all paths westward in the mid-1800s was the Oregon Trail. Starting in 1841, annual migrations to Oregon set out from Missouri. The trail was about 2,000 miles long, and the journey took four to six months. Many familiar images of pioneer travel date from the time of the Oregon Trail, including that of wagons arranged in a circle for defense against attack by Native Americans. It appears, however, that this particular threat was actually minimal. Native Americans reportedly were reluctant to attack a big, well-defended wagon train. The Oregon Trail continued to be used through the 1880s.

The leading edges of the westward movement became known as the frontier. The legacy of the American frontier included countless deaths; a despoiled landscape; and the subjugation of indigenous

Along the Oregon Trail, about halfway to Fort Vancouver, the well-known landmark Independence Rock rose up along the north bank of the Sweetwater River. Here settlers stopped their wagons for water and exchanged information about conditions farther west.

peoples. A huge new mythology was created, including characters such as Davy Crockett, Daniel Boone, the fictional logger Paul Bunyan, and a long list of colorful place names such as Bearmouth, Bonanza, Bumble Bee, Chloride, Cornucopia, Eureka, Gem, Giltedge, Gold Hill, Gold Point, Greenhorn, Malheur (unhappiness) City, Rattlesnake Haven, Rough and Ready, Ruby Gulch, Silver Reef, Tombstone, and Volcano.

Another legacy of the frontier was a particular mentality that did much to shape American thinking and society, according to historian Frederick Jackson Turner (1861–1932). In a paper published in 1893, "The Significance of the Frontier in American History," Turner argued that many outstanding characteristics of American life originated on the frontier. They included a keen and inquisitive intelligence; a practical attitude; an ability to master the material world and do great things both in and with it; and a "restless, nervous energy."

19

In other words, the frontiersman was an energetic explorer who got things done and then was on to his next big project.

Turner's argument was actually more complex than this. In short, however, he maintained that the frontier mind-set did much to shape the "psychology" of Uncle Sam. In this way, supposedly, the stereotype originated of the expansive, driven, tinkering American who believed that any problem could be solved, and that an American was the person to solve it.

Turner had his critics. Not everyone accepted his claims. He was faulted for paying too little attention, for example, to the contributions of blacks and Native Americans to American society. In many respects, however, Turner's frontier theory is now seen as correct. From the frontier came many of the traits, institutions, habits, ideals, and myths that guided—for better or worse—the development of 20th-century America.

Turner's thesis is reflected in our lives today. Under the skin, we are still a frontier people, and the frontier environment of generations long dead continues to influence us as individuals and as a society, even in an age of satellites, lasers, and desktop computers.

The Indian Wars

PIONEERS DID NOT SIMPLY SWEEP INTO THE WEST unopposed. Native Americans put up a fight for the lands that they considered their own. This lengthy string of battles and campaigns has gone down in history under the name of the "Indian wars."

The eventual outcome of the Indian wars was never seriously in doubt. The Native Americans were bound to lose. They faced an enemy that was much greater in number and also better armed. The easterners were backed by a more advanced technology, as well as the resources of a powerful manufacturing base and economic system. Moreover, the easterners were committed not only to pushing Native Americans off the land but also to destroying, in many cases, the animal populations on which Native American society depended for survival—in particular, the buffalo.

Nonetheless, the Native Americans managed to resist and sometimes temporarily stop the invasion from the East. Much of the actual fighting occurred on the Great Plains. When the U.S. Army tried to relocate Native Americans there to reservations to make way

A Lakota Sioux encampment during the late 19th century. By this time, Native American communities were under great stress, having been removed from their traditional lands and onto reservations.

for new settlements and railroads, the soldiers had to confront the formidable warriors of the Plains peoples.

Well-armed and expert horsemen, the Plains tribes were also powerfully motivated to fight for their homeland. They could not be swept aside easily. A case in point is the so-called Fetterman massacre near Fort Phil Kearny in Wyoming on December 21, 1866. Warriors

Today, small herds of bison survive in game preserves, but in earlier times their numbers covered the Great Plains. Buffalo hunters slaughtered them by the thousands. Their meat fed soldiers, miners, and settlers, and their hides were shipped back East to provide the leather belts that ran industrial machinery. With the disappearance of the buffalo, the Indians lost their source of food, clothing, and housing material. The nomadic life of the Plains Indians was based on the migrations of the buffalo, and disappeared with them.

Geronimo, the Apache chief who shunned reservation life and fought both Mexicans and Americans to remain free, photographed in 1887.

from the Arapaho, Cheyenne, and Sioux peoples completely wiped out a detachment of 80 soldiers commanded by Brevet Lieutenant Colonel William Fetterman.

The Sioux had already scored a notable win over the army the previous year during the Powder River expedition in 1865. Under the command of General Patrick Connor, this military expedition aimed to halt raids by Sioux and Cheyenne on roads running through the native peoples' hunting areas. The expedition was poorly equipped and failed miserably. Its bedraggled remnants had to be led back to a fort by Pawnee scouts. The Powder River debacle represented both a military and a psychological victory for Native Americans.

Conditions in the army actually helped the Native Americans to some extent. They were fighting not a uniformly brave,

Hunkpapa Sioux chief Sitting Bull, photographed in 1869 with his mother, daughter, and grandson.

The Santee Sioux of Minnesota had ceded their lands to the U.S. government in 1851, becoming entirely dependent on federal grants for their survival. When the government failed to pay them in 1862, they rioted and killed about 800 white settlers before they were captured. Pictured here are white survivors of the Indian raids, assembled for removal to safety at Fort Ridgely.

well-equipped, and well-disciplined army—as some works of fiction might have us believe—but rather a troubled army that bore little resemblance to the fighting force of today.

At the time of the Indian wars, army life was harsh. Soldiers' pay was next to nothing. Drunkenness was widespread. Discipline was severe and many soldiers deserted. This handicapped army had to wage war against the highly mobile and motivated Native American warriors, who had the advantage of fighting on their own territory.

After the army's slaughter of Sioux at Wounded Knee Creek in 1890, about 4,000 Sioux established a large encampment to protect themselves near White Clay Creek on the South Dakota–Nebraska border, in defiance of the government's efforts to make them return to the Pine Ridge Agency. By combining diplomacy with threats of force, General Nelson A. Miles induced the Sioux to surrender.

To make matters worse for the army, fighting did not occur on a clearly defined front, and the army could not adapt easily to such fluid conditions.

Some campaigns against native peoples were especially difficult for the army. An example is the Modoc war, which occurred from

A mountain of more than 200,000 buffalo hides at Dodge City, Kansas, in 1874. The most effective way of driving the Indians off their lands and forcing them onto reservations was to destroy their source of food.

The Battle of the Washita in November 1868. In retaliation for raids on white settlements in Kansas, troops of George Armstrong Custer's Seventh Cavalry descended on the Oklahoma camp of Chief Black Kettle and killed 140 people before being forced to withdraw as reinforcements from neighboring tribes arrived.

1872 to 1873. The Modoc people lived in southern Oregon and northern California. In a move reminiscent of the "tunnel war" in Vietnam some 100 years later, the Modoc people took refuge in the Lava Beds volcanic formation near Tule Lake, California. The land there was riddled with natural tunnels left by streams of lava that flowed underground long ago. Protected by this natural hideout, the Modoc held out for months against the army. On January 17, 1873, 50 Modoc warriors defeated an army force six times larger in size. The Modoc war cost the U.S. government more than half a million dollars, a huge sum at that time. (There were periods in the 1860s when the entire federal treasury contained less than $1 million.)

Much of the power of the northern Plains Indians was destroyed in the military campaign of 1876 to 1877. The army had to fight a massive force of several thousand warriors. The famous Colonel

George Armstrong Custer and the troops under his command were killed during this campaign at the Little Bighorn River in Montana on June 25, 1876.

The popular image of the bloodthirsty, treacherous "savage," scalping and murdering white men, women, and children, has some

Gold was discovered in the Black Hills of South Dakota in 1874, and the government pressed the Sioux to allow miners and settlers onto ancestral lands guaranteed to them by treaty. The Sioux war chief Crazy Horse refused to cooperate, and on June 17, 1876, his warriors defeated troops under General George Cook at the Battle of the Rosebud River, pictured here. Eight days later, on June 25, Crazy Horse's warriors wiped out more than 200 troopers of Custer's Seventh Cavalry at the Little Bighorn River.

basis in fact. Reports from the Kansas frontier in the late 1860s, for example, describe in detail the slaughter of white settlers. A case in point is the terror campaign that Chief Dull Knife and his band of northern Cheyenne raiders conducted in Kansas in 1878. These Cheyenne raids allegedly killed several dozen pioneers before the raiders were finally subdued.

On the other hand, it was not unheard-of for a white settler to go to considerable trouble and risk to save Native Americans from persecution. Historian Joanna Stratton, in her history of women on the Kansas frontier, tells of the day one Mrs. Campbell of Salina saw two natives running toward her home with soldiers in pursuit. Without hesitating, she quickly took in the natives. The soldiers, who were drunk, knocked on the door and threatened to shoot if Mrs. Campbell did not produce the natives. Mrs. Campbell refused to comply and threatened to shoot back. Rebuffed, the soldiers left. "No forget, white sister!" the thankful natives said upon leaving.

The Apache were among the last Native American peoples to be subdued in the Indian wars. Apache warriors operated in small bands and conducted, for years, a successful resistance against government forces. One of the greatest Apache warriors was Geronimo (1829–1909), whose actual name was Goyakla, or "the Yawner." Geronimo operated on both sides of the U.S.–Mexican border in a spectacular campaign of resistance that lasted almost 10 years. Government efforts to subdue the Apaches involved more than 40 companies of U.S. infantry and cavalry. All of this activity was aimed at defeating a band of only several dozen warriors. In the end, Geronimo surrendered to the U.S. military in 1886. He wound up working as a rancher around the time of his death.

A fanciful engraving of George Armstrong Custer's death struggle at the Battle of the Little Bighorn on June 25, 1876.

Another famous figure of the Indian wars was the Apache leader Cochise (1824–1874). Tall and impressive, Cochise led a campaign of terror through Arizona and portions of Mexico between 1861 and 1872. His war on settlers in the United States started after he was falsely accused of kidnapping a white child in Arizona. (Apache raiders had indeed kidnapped the child, but Cochise was not responsible for that crime.)

The story of Cochise's surrender in 1874 is a colorful bit of Western lore. Cochise is said to have trusted only one white man, a stagecoach operator named Thomas Jeffords. When the U.S. government decided to try making peace with the Apache leader, Jeffords was sent to meet with Cochise at the warrior's hideout in the Dragoon Mountains of Arizona. Jeffords went in alone. His courage in doing so impressed

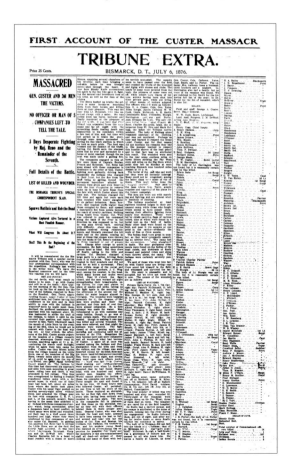

The front page of the July 6, 1876, edition of the *Bismarck Tribune* reported the deaths of Custer and the men of the Seventh Cavalry and asked what the government would do about it. Ironically, this Indian victory incensed Congress, overwhelmed the objections of eastern reformers to the way the Indians were treated, and led to the military campaigns that finally crushed Native American resistance in the West.

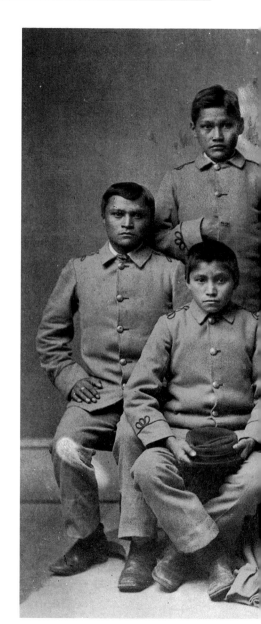

A group of Chiricahua Apache after four months of training at the Indian school in Carlisle, Pennsylvania, in 1886. Even many reform-minded whites believed that the answer for Indian survival was to adopt the white man's ways—his religion, his dress, his language. After arrival at Carlisle, the Apache had their hair cut and their names changed.

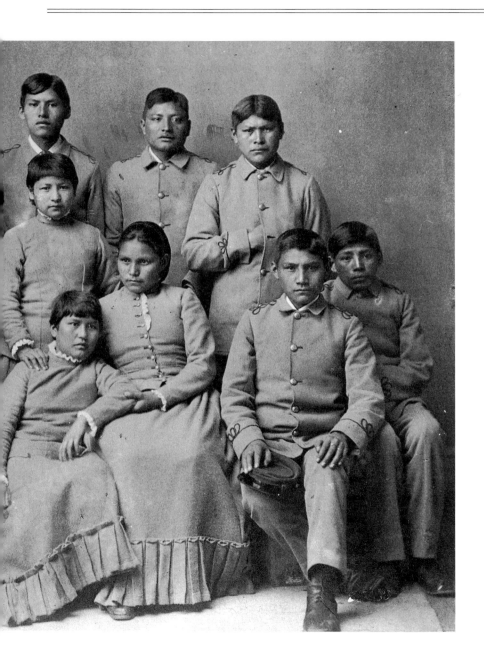

Cochise so greatly that the whites and the Apaches under Cochise's leadership were able to reach an agreement. The Native Americans received the large Chiricahua reservation in southern Arizona. The reservation was created by executive order in 1872. Jeffords became the Indian agent for the reservation. However, the executive order was revoked only four years later, and the Chiricahua Apache on the reservation were relocated.

The Indian wars ended with the Wounded Knee Massacre on December 29, 1890. The army encountered resistance from the Sioux at Wounded Knee Creek, South Dakota, following the death of the great Sioux leader Sitting Bull. There is disagreement about which side opened fire first. The dead included 146 Indians and 25 army men.

Despite the carnage of the Indian wars, the Native Americans had articulate and influential friends among whites, whose words and deeds introduced at least some compassion and moderation into a tragic chapter in American history. Yet however good the whites' intentions might be, Native Americans still tended to lose when those intentions were put into practice.

Perhaps the most prominent advocate for Native Americans in the nation's capital during the late 1800s was Henry Laurens Dawes (1816–1903), who represented Massachusetts in both the House of Representatives and the Senate between 1857 and 1893. Dawes took strong exception to America's rough treatment of its native peoples. While serving as chairman of the Senate Committee on Indian Affairs, Dawes began working toward what would become the Dawes Severalty Act of 1887.

This legislation was meant to help Native Americans by granting them plots of land on reservations for farming and grazing. The

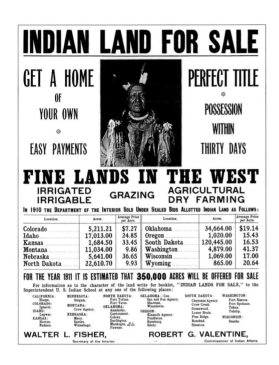

INDIAN LAND FOR SALE

GET A HOME
OF
YOUR OWN
❋
EASY PAYMENTS

PERFECT TITLE
❋
POSSESSION
WITHIN
THIRTY DAYS

FINE LANDS IN THE WEST

IRRIGATED
IRRIGABLE   GRAZING   AGRICULTURAL
DRY FARMING

IN 1910 THE DEPARTMENT OF THE INTERIOR SOLD UNDER SEALED BIDS ALLOTTED INDIAN LAND AS FOLLOWS:

Location.	Acres.	Average Price per Acre.	Location.	Acres.	Average Price per Acre.
Colorado	5,211.21	$7.27	Oklahoma	34,664.00	$19.14
Idaho	17,013.00	24.85	Oregon	1,020.00	15.43
Kansas	1,684.50	33.45	South Dakota	120,445.00	16.53
Montana	11,034.00	9.86	Washington	4,879.00	41.37
Nebraska	5,641.00	36.65	Wisconsin	1,069.00	17.00
North Dakota	22,610.70	9.93	Wyoming	865.00	20.64

FOR THE YEAR 1911 IT IS ESTIMATED THAT **350,000** ACRES WILL BE OFFERED FOR SALE

For information as to the character of the land write for booklet, "INDIAN LANDS FOR SALE," to the Superintendent U. S. Indian School at any one of the following places:

CALIFORNIA:	MINNESOTA:	NORTH DAKOTA:	OKLAHOMA—Con.	SOUTH DAKOTA:	WASHINGTON:
Hoopa.	Onigum.	Fort Totten.	Sac and Fox Agency.	Cheyenne Agency.	Fort Simcoe.
COLORADO:		Fort Yates.	Shawnee.	Crow Creek.	Fort Spokane.
Ignacio.	MONTANA:	OKLAHOMA:	Wyandotte.	Greenwood.	Tekoa.
IDAHO:	Crow Agency.	Anadarko.		Lower Brule.	Tulalip.
Lapwai.	NEBRASKA:	Cantonment.	OREGON:	Pine Ridge.	WISCONSIN:
KANSAS:	Macy.	Colony.	Klamath Agency.	Rosebud.	Oneida.
Horton.	Santee.	Darlington.	Pendleton.	Sisseton.	
Nadeau.	Winnebago.	Muskogee, etc.	Roseburg.		
		Pawnee.	Siletz.		

WALTER L. FISHER, Secretary of the Interior.   ROBERT G. VALENTINE, Commissioner of Indian Affairs.

As late as the early 1900s, as this advertisement shows, the government was selling to whites Indian lands that were supposedly protected by treaty.

Dawes Act also opened up Indian land, however, for purchase by whites. What happened afterward was a calamity for the natives. Their land holdings diminished by more than half within 50 years after the Dawes Act's passage. In 1887, Native Americans held more than 130 million acres. That figure dropped to less than 50 million acres by 1934.

Assimilation was another goal that white society had for Native Americans in the 19th century. Whites wanted to incorporate Native Americans into the predominantly Protestant culture of the East, and schools were set up on reservations for that purpose. Boarding schools also were established, far from reservations. The students, it was hoped, would adopt the ways of whites and enter the mainstream of white civilization. This effort was largely unsuccessful. Like oil and water, the two cultures simply did not mix.

The end of the last Indian wars involved, in a sense, the end of the American frontier. According to one definition, the frontier had marked the westward progress of settlement by easterners. At the close of the Indian wars, that expansion from the East had reached the Pacific coast of North America. There was simply nowhere left to go. The native peoples had been destroyed or displaced. The West had been opened, and the frontier was suddenly a thing of the past. Americans of European descent now dominated the whole country, from border to border and ocean to ocean.

As a cultural and political influence, however, the frontier was and still is very much alive. Frontier life in the 19th century has exerted a powerful influence on American culture to the present day. As a nation, we are descended in large part from the frontier mining towns, cattle towns, and farm communities of the 1800s. They represented a world and way of life very different from what we know today, but they also did much to make modern American society what it is.

Miners, Farmers, and Ranchers

SETTLERS EXPLOITED THE AMERICAN WEST IN THREE principal ways: mining, farming, and ranching. Each line of work gave rise to a certain way of life and a particular kind of community, with its own values and institutions.

Frontier towns had a wild reputation that is perhaps not entirely deserved. They were not populated solely by cowboys, gunslingers, prospectors, gamblers, and prostitutes. Successful frontier towns had many features in common with other communities of similar size in the East. There were schools, churches, restaurants, libraries, hotels, and various fraternal organizations.

Yet frontier towns also had their dark and violent side. On one occasion, the Park City, Utah, *Record* noted that there was too much "promiscuous" gunplay in the town's streets at night. Life appears to have been especially brutal in Vulture City, Arizona, where crimes such as murder and robbery reportedly occurred so often that 19 or more men were hanged from a single tree in the town plaza.

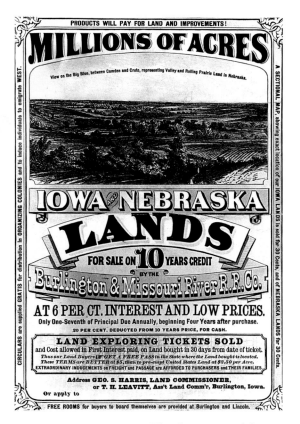

During the middle of the 19th century, millions of poor immigrants from Europe made the journey west to establish homesteads. Railroads acquired enormous amounts of land from the government in exchange for extending tracks into the new territories, and they sold this land to settlers to promote the building of communities that would be served by their lines.

The history of frontier towns is full of flamboyant figures, such as the lady known as "Captain" Jack. Her actual name was Ellen, and she made her home in Pitkin, Colorado. Rough, tough, and tenderhearted all at once, she would turn a gun on a man who displeased her, but hated to see animals suffer. According to one account, she once saw a man driving burros who were braying in pain because the driver was letting their loads rub their backs raw. Outraged, the "Captain" forced him at gunpoint to remove the poor animals' packs.

An early frontier home, made of sod bricks and a sod roof. It was truly a hard, primitive life. The only light for nighttime activities was provided by candles and oil lamps. During periods of unsettled weather, family members would take turns staying up at night, watching the horizon for lightning. A prairie wildfire could sweep across a farm family's homestead in a matter of minutes and wipe out everything they had.

In Perry, Oklahoma, in 1893, a crowd gathers in front of the local land office. The first land grants came as soon as there was a government, right after the revolutionary war, when veterans of the Continental army were pensioned off with land in the Ohio Valley. During the Civil War, Congress passed the Homestead Act, which granted 160—acre plots to anyone who would live on the land and farm it for five years. Similar land—distribution schemes continued throughout the 19th century.

Water was a precious commodity on the frontier. One story tells of a miner from Tombstone, Arizona, who was puzzled when a waitress in a restaurant in nearby Contention City placed a glass of water before him. "What is it?" the miner reportedly asked. When told it was water, he admitted that he had heard of it. "Even took a bath in it once," he added. He asked the waitress to put the water in a bottle so he could take it home and show it to his friends. The dry western

A group of gold miners in the Auburn Ravine, California, in 1852. The discovery of gold in California in 1848 led to a vast influx of settlers. Only a few struck it rich, but those who did not became California's farmers, merchants, and tradesmen.

countryside also figures in many other bits of mining-town lore. With tongue firmly in cheek, a newspaperman in Salome, California, once reported how a frog supposedly chased the cloud of smoke from a dynamite explosion for two miles, hoping it would rain. Less amusing was "miner's consumption," a lung disease caused by breathing in large amounts of dust. The dust hung in the air because mining operations had to be conducted without water for drills and crushers, and the dry earth around the mines was stirred up rather than held within cakes of mud.

As a rule, mining towns originated as a small cluster of buildings—shacks and frame houses, with a few stone or brick structures—in a lonely spot where water was scarce and the climate was severe. Smoke from smelters or mines hung over the community. The mining towns exhibited a characteristic life cycle. First there was a boom phase, when the town grew rapidly over a period of perhaps four or five years. The boom could not last indefinitely, however, and was soon followed by a slump. What happened next was either gradual extinction or a rebound made possible by new mining technology and an inflow of capital. When conditions favored growth, a mining camp could develop quickly into a relatively large, prosperous city. Less favored communities died and become "ghost towns." Deserted remains of many such towns can still be found in the western states.

Although the western mines yielded many different metals in the 19th century, the word "mining" then was synonymous with gold in many people's minds. "Gold fever" did perhaps as much as anything else to entice easterners to move westward. Only a small number of prospectors and other gold seekers, however, ever found any significant amount of the metal.

Prospectors panning for gold in Rockville, South Dakota. In two years, between 1876 and 1878, this region alone yielded more than $350,000 worth of gold.

Once gold was mined and refined, a problem arose—how to get the gold bullion out of town and deliver it to the mint. Bandits made that problem serious. At Kendall, Montana, for example, bandits knew when gold was about to leave town because the smelter used to refine the gold would emit a loud roar that indicated bullion was being processed. The people of Kendall became experts at concealing

45

gold shipments on the three stagecoach lines that served the town, according to historian Lambert Florin in his book *Guide to Western Ghost Towns.* The gold might be concealed in a passenger's trunk or even stashed in a sack sitting in plain view aboard a buggy.

This "hide-in-plain-sight" tactic once protected a shipment of $50,000 in gold, Florin writes. The gold was left sitting overnight in a bag on a counter at a clothing store in Lewistown, Montana, because

Turning the sod in Sun River, Montana, 1908. In another ten years or so, these horses would go to the slaughterhouse to be replaced by the first crude gasoline-powered tractors.

The fever for gold is dramatically depicted in this photograph of miners and prospectors hiking over the Chilcoot Pass to get to the Yukon Territory and Alaska. Few got rich, and many did not survive the journey.

the store's proprietor simply forgot to put it in the safe. That night, thieves who knew about the shipment broke into the store. They blasted open the safe, evidently presuming that the gold would be there. The robbers netted $200 from the safe, but the $50,000 in gold remained perfectly secure in the sack on the counter.

47

Drug abuse was also a problem in mining towns. The drug of choice was usually alcohol, but opium dens could also be found. In Mineral Park, Arizona, for example, several opium dens were active by 1884. The community tried to ignore the opium dens, but soon recognized that turning one's back would not make the problem go away. More and more young people became addicts. After a local newspaper, the *Mohave Miner,* began a crusade against the opium dens, they evidently disappeared.

Farm life during days on the frontier has been highly romanticized. By modern standards, it was actually a rugged, dangerous, and unpleasant existence. Frontier homes tended to be tiny and overcrowded. Historian Joanna Stratton, in her account of what life was like for women on the Kansas frontier, describes one Emma Hill's visit to her neighbors, the Elliotts, at their home around 1873. The Elliotts lived in a shanty measuring about 10 by 12 feet. Into this tiny space—no bigger than a bedroom in a modest apartment today—were packed the five Elliotts, together with a bed, a stove, a table, a safe, and several chairs. Four guests were also visiting the Elliotts at the time. The dwelling was so crowded that Emma Hill could not enter at all.

Some prairie homes were built of sod, the tough, fibrous mat of soil and vegetation that covered the prairie. Sod provided insulation against summer's heat and winter's cold. Sod was also fire resistant—an important safety feature on the prairie, where lightning from powerful thunderstorms caused fires that could sweep across the dry land with great speed during the hot season, consuming everything that would burn. More primitive "dugout" homes, as their name indicates, were dug into the sides of hills. The dugout technique saved on building materials in a region where there were

(continued on page 53)

"Dime novels," as they were called, did much to popularize, and exaggerate, the exploits of western outlaws and the lawmen who brought them to justice.

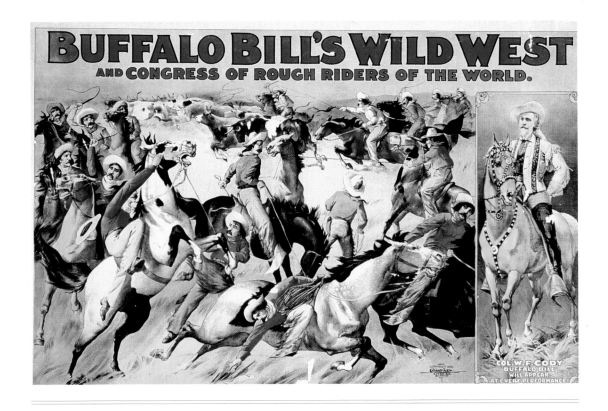

In the 1880s, Buffalo Bill's Wild West Show toured eastern cities and featured such legendary figures as Annie Oakley and Sitting Bull. Such shows also romanticized frontier life. It was all buffalo hunting, trick riding, and Indian fighting. The struggles of hardworking farmers and miners did not provide stories that were exciting enough for eastern tenderfeet.

Railroad building on the Great Plains. Railroads brought thousands of new settlers westward. They were perhaps not as hardy as the first generation of pioneers who came by wagon train, but they were just as anxious to start their own farms and ranches. The railroads also linked western farmers to consumers in eastern markets, and vastly increased the prosperity of western communities as a result.

National guardsmen fight off striking railway workers in 1894. Bitter labor struggles became common in the West almost as soon as the railroads and mining companies arrived.

(continued from page 48)
few trees for lumber, but the dwellings were miserable. In rainy weather, a dirt floor would become a muddy mess, and snakes would invade the house.

The sod that served so well as building material, however, made planting crops difficult. Laced with the tough roots of the prairie grass, the sod was so resistant that several oxen and men were needed to push a plow through it. Once the crops were planted (primarily wheat, corn, and potatoes, although farmers tried other crops ranging from barley to tobacco), the farmers had to cope with ground squirrels who stole seeds, and with the ever-present threat of destructive weather. Hot winds could shrivel crops in a single day. Hail could wipe out a harvest within minutes. These calamities were very common, and a completely successful harvest appears to have been unusual. When weather or pests such as grasshoppers destroyed crops, farm families had to fall back on other enterprises such as poultry and dairy farming. Settlers could also supplement their diets by hunting buffalo and prairie chickens.

Though it is fashionable to think of the frontier as a land of "rugged individualists," self-sufficient loners were almost unknown, at least in the farming communities. On the contrary, cooperative effort was needed to keep the communities going because of the serious labor shortage. Hospitality was a prominent feature of frontier life. Frontier folk appear to have spent a large part of their time visiting one another. Strangers were also welcome at frontier homes. Even disreputable-looking wanderers could find a friendly reception and a place to sleep at frontier households. Stratton mentions a tall, peculiar-looking woman who approached a frontier home and asked to spend the night. The family instantly welcomed her in. Before the family arose the next morning, the woman was

53

The first buildings of Nevada City—a mining town—are hacked out of the wilderness in 1852.

gone. Only later did the family learn that the "woman" had been the notorious bandit Jesse James, traveling in disguise.

The cattle industry did much to shape western society in the latter part of the 19th century. Cattle were driven in vast numbers northward from Texas to be shipped by rail to markets in the East.

Denver, the center of the southwestern mining area of the United States, in 1866. The wealth that flowed into Denver from gold and silver mining operations made possible many fine buildings and a small class of the wealthy with the same cultural pretensions as easterners. On the other hand, as the lithograph shows, pigs wandered freely in the streets.

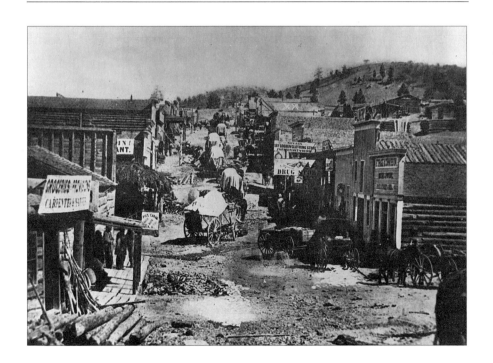

Farm families lived in isolation from each other and often at great distances from the nearest settlement. They were dependent on peddlers and traveling salesmen for many manufactured goods.

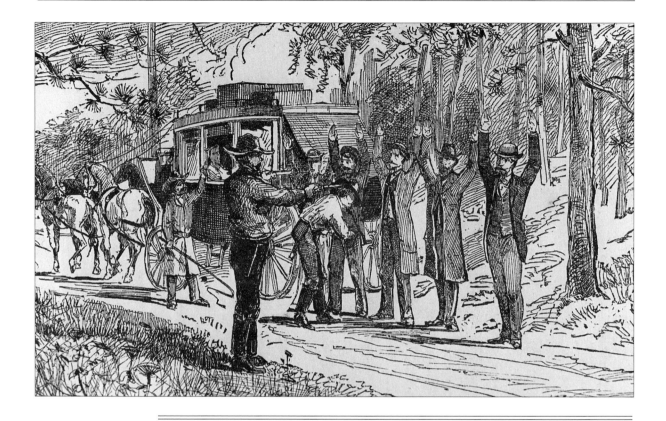

The "Mammoth Cave Stage Robbery," an etching from an early biography of Jesse James. Many former Civil War soldiers, mustered out with little money, their homes destroyed by the war, turned to banditry.

Cattle on these drives destroyed crops, thus generating great conflict between western farmers and cattlemen.

"Cattle towns" of the West arose and developed according to a pattern different from that of mining towns. A speculator or some other entrepreneur would sell land in a remote spot. As the local population grew and a community took shape, campaigns to bring in railroad lines would begin, in the hope of attracting the cattle business. When the cattle arrived, however, they ruined crops. Then farmers would call for a halt to the cattle business in that town, and in many cases the cattlemen had to retreat.

Cattle rustling was a widespread practice. Among the most prominent rustlers was one Ella Watson, who became known as "Cattle Kate." She was lynched, along with her partner Jim Averill, by ranchers in 1888. Cattle Kate's lynching was one of a number of incidents that led in 1892 to a cattle war in Wyoming, later known as the "Johnson County War."

Entertainment in frontier communities often involved cruelty to animals, as in dog fights and cock fights. When such games were not cruel, they were often ludicrous. At Nevada City, California, on one Fourth of July around 1850, word went out that the day's festivities would include a fight between a grizzly bear and a jackass. Two thousand spectators assembled outside town to watch the event. The "grizzly" turned out to be a young brown bear that was not in the mood for fighting at all. The bear approached the jackass in a friendly manner. The jackass responded by kicking the bear, who fled. The crowd then escorted the jackass back to Nevada City, drinking toasts to the animal at saloons along the way.

Most of us probably would not care to live under the conditions of 19th-century frontier life. The sheer amount of backbreaking labor necessary to keep a farm or ranch going, without modern machinery, seems almost inconceivable to us today. We have become too accustomed to modern conveniences such as indoor plumbing, automobiles, and washing machines. The pioneer farmer or rancher was also his own blacksmith, carpenter, and doctor. Yet it was the very harshness of life that created the core values Americans hold so dear—appreciation for honest work, willingness to innovate, and steadfastness in the face of difficult times.

The Populists and
the Silver Crusade

WHILE FRONTIER SOCIETY AND CULTURE DEVELOPED IN the 1800s, America as a whole was undergoing vast changes. The nation was being transformed by new industries and institutions such as railroads, which were connecting all corners of the United States. After about 1850, the country began to experience a rapidly shifting economic base as urban areas grew in size and more Americans began to work in industry than in agriculture.

In 1776, America had been as much an agrarian society as ancient Mesopotamia. A little more than a century later, America was about to change over from the plow to the piston; the horse was about to yield to the horseless carriage and the tractor; and political and economic power were about to shift away from rural areas to the major cities.

America in the late 19th century was dominated by the industrial states of the Northeast. Here were the new factories, the centers of banking, the stock markets, and the individuals who had made huge fortunes from America's expansion. Great rail lines extended out

This undated political cartoon depicts railroad magnate William Vanderbilt crushing the farmers and tradesmen of the western territories with the help of army troops. The railroads owned vast tracts of land and controlled the freight rates farmers had to pay to ship their goods back East. This financial strangulation gave rise to the populist movement in the West.

across the continent from the Northeast, linking city with country in an often uneasy association. In only a few decades, the nation had become sharply polarized between industry and agriculture; between city and country; and between the rich and the less affluent portions of society that remained closer to the land.

In earlier times, a transformation like this might have taken centuries and thus given society many generations to adapt. Now, however, great changes were compressed into a few years or even months. Even an adaptable society such as the United States had trouble adjusting to such rapid, sweeping developments.

No one felt the pace of change more keenly than the American farmer. In George Washington's day, the farmer was king. Ninety-five percent of Americans worked in agriculture in 1790. By 1910,

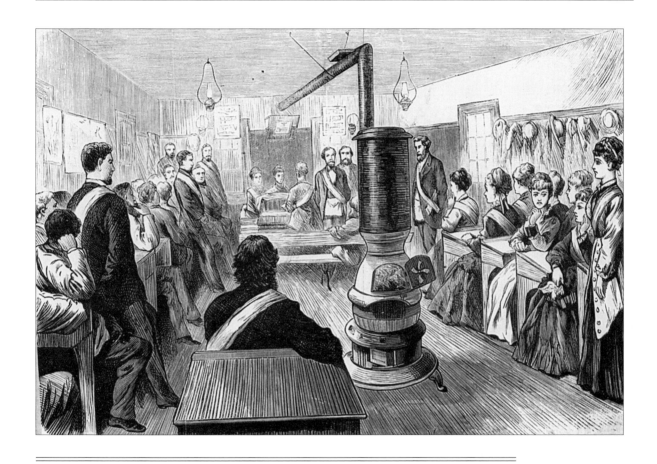

A meeting of the Grange in a western schoolhouse. The farmers who formed chapters of the National Order of Patrons of Husbandry fought for lower railroad freight rates, cheap land, cooperative marketing of farm products, and the easy credit policies associated with the free coinage of silver.

This 1873 political cartoon shows an iron horse, representing the railroad monopolies, eating all the corn out of a farmer's bin as he looks on in shock.

however, only 30 percent of Americans were farmers. (By 1985, only three percent of Americans listed their occupation as farmer or farm worker.)

Much as Native Americans had seen an invasion from the East wipe out their way of life, farmers in the second half of the 19th century became alarmed at perceived threats to their independence from the political and economic power of the industrialized East. Farmers were becoming the victims of exorbitant freight rates

charged by the railroads. The prices they were offered for their
harvests were controlled by commodities markets in Chicago,
Boston, or New York. The policies of eastern bankers and politicians
determined how easy or difficult it was for farmers to obtain credit
at planting time.

One result of all this dissatisfaction was the emergence of the
Populist movement, which grew out of farmers' efforts to elect local

At one point in its history, the Grange had almost a million members. In the town of Eagle
Rock, Idaho, in 1900, Grange cooperatives were wealthy enough to operate their own
grain-milling and farm-supply companies, freeing farmers from the clutches of middlemen.

William Jennings Bryan, the charismatic orator and politician who ran for the presidency several times on a populist program that included the free coinage of silver. His defeats in these presidential campaigns symbolized the waning political power of farmers as the nation experienced an industrial revolution in the late 19th century.

and national politicians committed to easy credit policies and the regulation of railroads. Populism was more than just a farmers' movement. It attracted tradesmen, social reformers, and urban workers who resented what they saw as ruthless exploitation by industrialists. The Populists wanted to see the "little man," as exemplified by the small farmer or individual worker, protected from abuse and exploitation by the more powerful elements of society. The Populists did not think that industries should be taken over by the state, as socialists would argue, but they did believe that laws should prevent the wealthy and powerful from exercising their influence unjustly over the poor and powerless.

This, of course, is something of an oversimplification. Populism was not a rigid doctrine with a well-organized group of adherents. Instead, it was a mood abroad in the country that encompassed many different attitudes and schools of thought on topics ranging from

An advertisement for an early–model washing machine. As farm families began to purchase more and more manufactured products, they became more dependent on the cash economy and less self-sufficient as farmers. This made them more sensitive to prices and interest rates, and more concerned with government policies that affected prices.

coinage to government regulation of industry. In general, however, populism could be summarized by saying, "Respect the little guy." In various forms, this core of populist belief exercised a great influence on American society in the late 19th and early 20th centuries.

The Populist movement had its roots in the National Grange and the Granger laws. The Grange was a loose-knit organization of farmers, founded in 1867 and dedicated to the formation of cooperatives that would give farmers more power in bargaining for better prices for their crops. As Grange members became powerful enough to elect political representatives, a number of laws were enacted to protect western farmers from arbitrary tariffs, high railroad freight rates, storage and handling fees by middlemen, and tight credit policies.

Farmers' discontent focused on the railroads, which charged too much and practiced discrimination in favor of big shippers. The farmers thought that the government should force the railroads to adopt policies more agreeable to farm interests. Discussions on such topics took place during Grange meetings, which also developed into social gatherings for farm communities. As Grange chapters helped draw attention to farmers' complaints, state legislatures took notice. In Illinois, Iowa, Wisconsin, and other western states, lawmakers passed legislation to bring railroad policies closer to what farmers favored. For example, the laws set maximum rates for freight and set up special commissions to enforce these laws.

The Granger laws were soon repealed under pressure from the railroads and industrialists, but the sentiments that produced them remained. Other agrarian movements arose in response to farmers' resentments. Prominent among them were the Farmers' Alliances,

68

(continued on page 73)

A meeting of Grange farmers in the woods near Winchester, Illinois, in 1873. The Grangers actively fought the railroads and the eastern bankers and monopolists, whose policies increased the costs of farming but held down the prices farmers received for their harvests.

A stagecoach and a Conestoga wagon sit in front of a country inn. This appears to be a genuine, full-sized Conestoga, built with a floor that slopes down toward the middle of the wagon, designed to keep freight from shifting over rough roads.

A lithograph showing a stagecoach of the California & Oregon Coach Company traveling through the Sierra Nevada, with Mount Shasta visible in the background.

Pioneers building a log cabin, from an illustration drawn around 1894.

A woodsman stops in the middle of a stream to water his packhorse, from an engraving by Frederic Remington. The true pioneers were these first mountain men and trailbreakers, who laid out the routes used by the wagon trains.

(continued from page 68)

which gave the Populist party its start. Known as the "people's party," the Populist party first emerged as a third political party to compete with the Democrats and Republicans on the state level in 1890. In that year's elections, Populists did not take control in any states but made a substantial showing at the polls.

A national Populist organization, under the name of the National People's party, was organized in 1891 and held its first nominating convention in Omaha, Nebraska, in 1892. The party platform called for the government takeover of railroads as well as telephone and telegraph systems. The platform also included demands for a monetary policy that would make it easier and cheaper to borrow money. Underlying much of the platform was the presumption—radical for its time—that government had a responsibility to look after the welfare of all its citizens, the weak and poor as well as the strong and wealthy.

The Populists made another good showing in the national election of 1892. What happened the following year helped to make Populist demands for currency reform an important issue nationwide. The stock market crash of 1893 marked the start of a painful depression. Although that decade has gone down in history as "the Gay Nineties," it actually was not a happy time. The nation would not see economic conditions as tough as these again until the Great Depression of the 1930s.

One-fifth of America's industrial workers were unemployed by the end of 1893. Tens of thousands of men in Chicago alone found themselves out of work. At the same time, prices for farm products dropped so low that farmers could not cover their costs of production. Families faced starvation as men and women were unable to find work anywhere.

73

An early harvester pulled by a team of 24 horses. Improvements in farm machinery enabled farmers to increase both the size of their farms and their productivity. But as the scale of their operations increased, so did the amount of capital they needed to keep their larger farms going. Increasing farm debt was another contributing factor to the Populist movement.

The depression brought the "silver issue" to the forefront. President Grover Cleveland blamed the depression on the Silver Purchase Act of 1873, which had eliminated silver dollars from U.S. currency. Previously, the United States had minted both gold and silver coins. Because silver was thought to be in greater supply than gold, Cleveland argued that repealing the Silver Purchase Act would end

Topeka, Kansas, in the 1890s. The frontier town had become a busy city with tall buildings, paved sidewalks, trolley cars, electric lights, and telephone lines.

Big industry and big business were new and frightening phenomena for most Americans in the 19th century, and were viewed with great suspicion. This cartoon from 1890 depicts the nation being swallowed by monopoly.

the depression by increasing the money supply. It seems unlikely that such a measure would have helped much, but the silver issue acquired a symbolism that had tremendous political impact. "Free silver," as the pro-silver cause was known, also symbolized a need for far-reaching reforms that would benefit the "common man" and protect him from exploitation by the wealthy.

The politically charged silver issue divided the country into two camps. "Goldbugs" favored a gold standard, while "silverites" wanted silver currency. Farmers, the mainstay of the Populist movement, favored free silver because they thought it would bring

Even urban centers felt the power of the new monopolies. This magazine sketch protests the control of the railroads over eastern port facilities.

them greater prosperity by putting more money in circulation. Propagandists for the pro-silver movement included William H. "Coin" Harvey, who wrote a highly successful tract called "Coin's Financial School." In Harvey's story, a "Professor Coin" explained the alleged benefits of free silver and revealed a conspiracy underlying those who supported the gold standard. Then, as now, conspiracy theories evidently had a wide and appreciative audience.

In this cartoon from 1888, a farmer and a laborer carry a monopolist in a style reminiscent of European royalty.

In 1874, striking coal miners in Washingtonville, Ohio "serenade" a scab who has returned to work.

Populists eventually joined forces with the Democrats in the early 1890s, because by then the Populist party had achieved all it could by itself. In 1896, the Populists and Democrats together nominated the free-silver advocate, Nebraska politician William Jennings Bryan (1860–1925), as their candidate for president. Now remembered mainly for his role in the prosecution at the Scopes "monkey trial" of 1925, in which a Tennessee schoolteacher named John Scopes was tried for teaching the theory of evolution, Bryan was a skilled orator. He expounded the western, pro-silver view-point as a member of Congress in the early 1890s. He became famous for his eloquent "Cross of Gold" speech at the Democratic National Convention in 1896, in which he portrayed the gold-versus-silver issue as the crucifixion of humankind upon a golden cross. Bryan was known for turning Biblical imagery to political ends in his oratory.

The energetic Bryan traveled thousands of miles on the campaign trail in 1896, plugging the silver issue for all it was worth. Although he won the hearts and votes of the western and southern states, he could not sway enough voters in the Midwest and the Northeast, and so the Democrats under Bryan lost to the Republicans, led by

Government land grants to railroad companies were so generous that the railroads were able to offer the land for sale to settlers at bargain prices. This helped to build up the population of western communities, creating more business for the railroads.

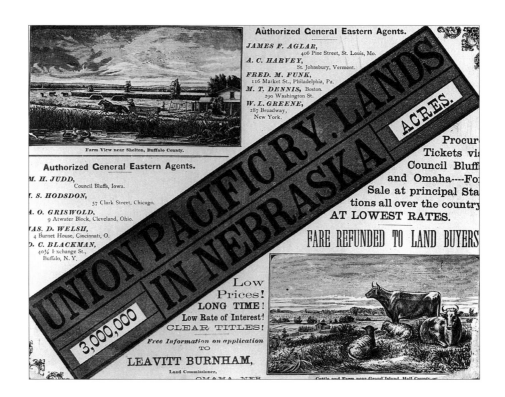

In 1881, a farm family poses with the primitive agricultural implements of the time. By the 1880s, some harvesting machines were powered by steam engines, but the horse and hand labor were still important.

William McKinley. Bryan ran again for president in 1900 and 1908, both times unsuccessfully. By the time he died in 1925, the political movement he had represented, the Populist crusade of the 1890s, had died as well.

Populism had its roots on the frontier, and as the agrarian-centered frontier culture vanished, so did the Populist party. Yet Populism's influence endured. Many politicians and political movements of the 20th century can trace their origins back to Populism by one route or another. America's modern welfare state is based on the Populist notion that government should assume responsibility for the welfare of its citizens, including the poor and powerless. In short, Populist ideals are still with us, even though the Populist party and the frontier environment that gave rise to it are long past. The old frontier may be gone, but its legacy lives on.

The Myth of the Frontier

AS WE SAW EARLIER, THE REALITIES OF FRONTIER LIFE WERE often harsh and unpleasant. The frontier was dangerous. Epidemic disease and death by violence were commonplace. Settlers had to work long and hard for their living, and the benefits of their labor could be wiped out in minutes by storms or fire. Warfare and terrorism occurred frequently. Even a harmless-looking tuft of grass might conceal death in the form of a rattlesnake.

What for us would be a brief, everyday journey to a nearby city or county could have been a perilous expedition 100 years ago. Most conveniences of modern life—even small but important items such as pesticides—simply did not exist then. In many areas, competent medical care was so distant that it might as well have been nonexistent.

In addition to everything else, frontier folk would have had to contend with boredom and depression to an extent that is hard to fathom today. We who live in a society filled with diversions find it difficult to imagine how boring and isolated life must have been

Frontier settlers in Minnesota. East of the Great Plains, farm families literally had to hack their fields out of the dense forests. Felling trees, uprooting stumps, moving stones, and turning the soil was backbreaking work for the whole family, and it took several years before the first good harvest came in. Those were lean years in which the family had to subsist by hunting and fishing.

in a sod home on the prairie in the late 1800s. Your small, crowded, smelly home is surrounded by flat, empty land, many miles from the nearest community. You have no transportation or long-distance communication faster than a horse. Television and radio do not exist. Drawing water means a hike to the nearest stream, carrying heavy buckets. Bathing is a luxury. So is anything even faintly resembling fashionable clothing. If something breaks, you have to fix it yourself. (You probably would have had to build it in the first place.)

Of course, modern life is by no means carefree, either. We are often bombarded by noise from police sirens, car alarms, and neighbors'

Typical of the independent western woman was Phoebe Anne Oakley Mozee, known as Annie Oakley. As the child of an Ohio farmer, she helped supplement the family income by shooting quail and rabbits and soon became an expert markswoman, able to hit a dime thrown into the air from 90 feet away. In 1885 she went to work for Buffalo Bill's Wild West Show at Louisville, Kentucky.

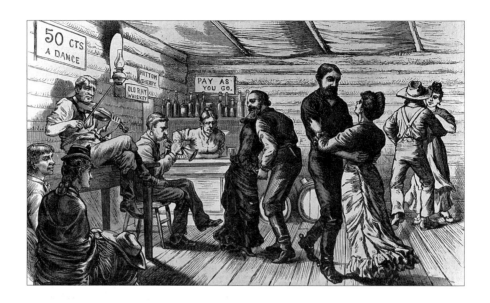

A dance hall in the mining town of Leadville, Colorado. Though their environment was rough and primitive, miners wanted the companionship of women. The desire for family life and the amenities of civil society would eventually tame the frontier.

stereos. City streets are dangerous. The mass media constantly tell us how unsafe life is becoming. Yet modern America probably would have seemed like paradise to a prairie dweller some 100 years ago.

All the same, a number of romantic fantasies have arisen concerning the history of the American frontier. Examples of frontier myths are visible all around us. For example, the dirty sod dwelling of the late 19th century becomes, in modern imagination, a clean, happy home filled with virtue and joy and surrounded by natural beauty. Hollywood films portray the settler's house as a fine log or wood structure. However, when the first settlers arrived on the Great Plains, they found no trees with which to build wooden houses. Myths minimize the harsh climate and the tough economic conditions that settlers found on the 19th-century frontier. Those conditions gave rise to songs with titles such as "Starving to Death on a Government Claim."

Not all the women on the frontier were of "respectable" character, as shown in this scene from a concert hall in Butte City, Montana.

A posed portrait of the Sioux war chief Sitting Bull standing next to Buffalo Bill, photographed some time around 1885. After the Sioux had been driven from their traditional lands onto reservations, Sitting Bull surrendered to the army and eventually went to work in Buffalo Bill's Wild West Show.

A group of actresses on a tour of mining camps pose in hiking gear. Such traveling shows were greatly appreciated by the miners, who often spent months isolated in their remote camps.

Much of the mythology of the frontier had its origins in 19th-century "dime novels." These stories sold for 10 cents each and were the ancestors of 20th-century pulp magazines and paperback books. Dime novels originated just before the War Between the States. They were quick reads—perhaps an hour from cover to cover—and in some cases sold millions of copies.

Perhaps the influence of dime novels on western lore and popular culture can be seen best in the career of William F. "Buffalo Bill" Cody (1846–1917), an Iowa-born army scout. In life, Cody appears to have been a highly competent scout and a good marksman. In legend, after dime novels had done their work, he became the practical embodiment of the frontier hero. In the 1860s, the then-obscure Cody came to the attention of an author named Edward Judson, whose

An advertisement for a popular drama about western lawmen and gunslingers. Such plays were popular in the West as well as the East, though they greatly romanticized life on the frontier.

In 1873, Grangers rally in Edwardsville, Illinois, before a meeting.

sensational account of Cody's life, "Buffalo Bill, King of Border Men," was published in a New York journal in 1869. Thereafter, Cody figured in more than 1,000 dime novels. His life became so encrusted with fiction that sometimes one could scarcely tell where fact ended and fantasy began. (His life was often at odds with his reputation. For example, he was famed for slaughtering great numbers of buffalo but appears actually to have killed only a few of them.)

Buffalo Bill's traveling Wild West Show, which began in 1883, contributed to the mythology of the frontier. One of the acts included a dramatization of an attack on a stagecoach. Among Cody's

Pioneers journey westward in a covered wagon pulled by oxen. In the early days, horses were too expensive for most settlers, and oxen pulled the wagons and plows of the poorer farmers.

performers was sharpshooter Annie Oakley. Even the great Sioux leader Sitting Bull made an appearance with Cody's show. Cody's extravaganza and others like it contributed to a blend of fact and romantic falsehood that had a profound effect on popular views of the frontier.

For example, dime novels and Wild West shows glamorized the cowboy. Nowhere has mythology overlapped history more

When in 1829 Andrew Jackson was elected president, it was considered a victory for the small farmer, workingman, and tradesman. So jubilant were his supporters that they mobbed and looted the White House during the inauguration ceremony.

This illustration makes the point that the farmer supports all the other professions of society—lawyers, politicians, doctors, soldiers, and merchants.

completely than in cowboy lore. Popular entertainment in our own time represents the cowboy as a young white male in exotic clothing, singing ballads about his lonely life and shooting up the landscape with his revolver.

There is some truth in this picture, but not much. Not all cowboys, for example, were white. About one out of every five cowboys was black. Some cowboys were Native Americans. Also, gunplay among cowboys appears to have been rare. They were not, as a rule, gunslingers. Cowboys were professionals with a job to do. Their work was exhausting, frequently brutal, and often performed in conditions of intense heat or cold. Cowboys had a monotonous diet (largely bacon, beans, and bread) and little chance for rest. It is hard to imagine a life farther removed from the legend of the "singing cowboy" riding the range and serenading his horse.

Nonetheless, the fanciful, dime-novel image of cowboys has endured and evolved. Hollywood took it up and based countless motion pictures upon it. Radio and television also did their best to exploit cowboy lore. The results were entertaining and sometimes bizarre, in the tradition of the dime novel and the Wild West show.

The mythology of the frontier survives in the dreams and rhetoric of our day. In the early 1960s, for example, the administration of President John F. Kennedy called its agenda the "New Frontier." This expression brought to mind exciting images of unexplored lands waiting to be conquered, despite the fact that the frontier, in a geographical sense, had been closed for half a century. In this context, it is worth noting that the Western was one of the most popular genres of television shows during the 1960s.

Moreover, America's frontier mythology underwent a dramatic transformation on TV during the late 1960s, when the famous television series *Star Trek* projected the American frontier into the future and out into the galaxy. Popular entertainment was never the same again.

Even today, one easy way to lend glamour to something is to describe it as a "frontier." That trick works because deep down we are still frontier folk. Even lifelong city dwellers have a warm place in their hearts for the frontier. As Frederick Jackson Turner observed,

As late as 1900, this upstate New York farm family had no other way to get to town than to hitch their cows to their primitive mechanical harvester.

the old frontier culture made us what we are today. It is part of our national character; and a nation's character resists change.

Yet sometimes change is needed. In the years ahead, we may have to ask ourselves if the frontier mythology is, on balance, a good thing. Is it mere escapism, based on old dreams that have no place in modern times? Does the myth of the frontier encourage us to run from problems in the here and now and flee toward some imagined wilderness, in a mistaken belief that life there will be happier? Perhaps it does, too often. This is not to say that exploration, investigation, and discovery should stop. "Out there," on some frontier of knowledge and experimentation, we may find solutions to many pressing problems. But the old western frontier, in any case, is gone. It now exists only in our minds and hearts.

FURTHER READING

Billington, Ray. *America's Frontier Heritage.* Albuquerque: University of New Mexico Press, 1974.

Dykstra, Robert. *Cattle Towns.* New York: Atheneum, 1970.

Florin, Lambert. *Guide to Western Ghost Towns.* Superior, WI: Superior Publications, 1976.

Hicks, John D. *The Populist Revolt: A History of the Farmers' Alliance and the People's Party.* Westport, CT: Greenwood Publishing Group, 1981.

Hofstadter, Richard. *The Age of Reform: From Bryan to F. D. R.* New York: Vintage Books, 1955.

Knight, Oliver. *Following the Indian Wars.* Norman: University of Oklahoma Press, 1960.

Lamar, Howard, ed. *Reader's Encyclopedia of the American West.*
New York: Crowell Press, 1978.

Russell, Don. *The Wild West: A History of the Wild West Shows.*
New York: Abrams, 1971.

INDEX

PICTURE CREDITS

DAVID RITCHIE is the author of numerous nonfiction books, including *The Computer Pioneers: a History of Early Electronic Computers*, and the *Encyclopedia of Earthquakes and Volcanoes*. He lives in Baltimore, Maryland.